The handy band

Supporting **Personal**, **Social** and **Emotional Development**
with new songs from old favourites

Sue Nicholls

with illustrations by Carol Jonas
cover by Alex Ayliffe

A ⬛⬛⬛ n

D0714113

07·07

For Alice, Jack and Brian

First published 2004 by
A&C Black Publishers Ltd
37 Soho Square
London W1D 3QZ

Text © 2004 Sue Nicholls
Cover design by Jocelyn Lucas
Cover illustration © 2004 Alex Ayliffe
Inside design by Carla Moss
Inside illustrations © 2004 Carol Jonas
Edited by Marie Penny and
Sheena Roberts

A&C Black uses paper produced with
elemental chlorine-free pulp, harvested
from managed sustainable forests.

Printed in Great Britain by
Martins the Printers Ltd
Berwick upon Tweed

ISBN 0-7136-6897-0

The author and publishers would like to thank
the following people for their help in preparing
this book: Sally Hickman, Paul Hopkins, Cath
Rasbash, Helen Sampson, Jane Sebba and
Emily Wilson.

Introduction

The handy band is a collection of thirty new songs set to familiar tunes, with a sprinkling of raps and chants. It provides the generalist practitioner with an accessible musical support for delivering Physical, Emotional and Social Development (PSED) at the Foundation Stage. PSED is one of the six areas for learning in the QCA's Curriculum Guidance for the Foundation Stage in England – this is in common with the Foundation Stage in Wales, Scotland and Northern Ireland.

The structure of the book

The material in **The handy band** is divided into six sections:

Dispositions and attitudes;

Self-confidence and self-esteem;

Making relationships;

Behaviour and self-control;

Self-care;

Sense of community.

Each section contains five songs with ideas for using the song and suggestions for activities which are matched to a PSED focus. The sections mirror the breakdown of the whole area of Physical, Emotional and Social Development within the Guidance.

The songs, raps and chants provide a wide range of subjects for circle time and should promote lively discussion opportunities for practitioners to share with their children.

A holistic approach

Combining music with PSED reflects a holistic approach to the Foundation Stage Curriculum. Many of the songs and chants use actions, puppets or role-play to underpin this area of learning.

About the melodies

As a quick reminder of the melodies, the opening notes of each one are given on the page in letter form using this system:

D͵ E͵ F͵ G͵ A͵ B͵ C D E F G A B C¹
(low)   (middle)   (high)

The dashes above or below the letter indicate a higher or lower pitch. These can be played on chime bars, a xylophone or glockenspiel. The complete melodies, raps and chants are given in staff notation at the back of the book. If a tune is unknown to you, someone who can read music will be able to teach it to you.

Bring a new dimension to your PSED with these simple and expressive songs, raps and chants and enjoy the opportunity to engage your children with some new musical experiences.

Sue Nicholls

Contents

 **Dispositions and attitudes**

Self-confidence and self-esteem

Making relationships

Behaviour and self-control

Self-care

Sense of community

1 First day

Tune: Knees up, Mother Brown

Are you feeling new?
We know what to do,
Build a castle,
Build a castle,
Making friends with you.

Are you feeling new?
We know what to do,
Tell a story,
Tell a story,
Making friends with you.

PSED focus Helping children to become familiar with their new setting.

Using the song Make up actions to go with each verse, eg 'build a castle' – place fist on fist; 'tell a story' – hold hands open like a book.

With the children, make up additional verses by listing other activities and, if appropriate, inventing actions for them.

B, D D D D
Are you feel - ing new?

2 Special things I do

Tune: John Brown's body

I like cartwheels,
   they're the special things I do,
I like cartwheels,
   they're the special things I do,
I like cartwheels,
   they're the special things I do,
So come and play with me.

  I can't do cartwheels,
    they are tricky things to do ...
  Let's go on the slide instead.

I like sewing, it's the special thing I do ...
So come and play with me.

  I can't do sewing, it's a tricky thing to do ...
  Let's play in the sand instead.

PSED focus Sharing, celebrating and discussing personal achievements.

Using the song Highlight individual children's special talents to show that some achievements are not yet manageable by everyone.

	D	D	C, B,	D
♪	I	like ____	cart-wheels	

3 Come for tea

Tune: A sailor went to sea, sea, sea

Please come and play with me, me, me,
And you can stay for tea, tea, tea.
There's sausages to eat, eat, eat,
'Cos they're my favourite treat, treat, treat!

    I'd really like to come, come, come,
    I'm thinking of my tum, tum, tum.
    But sausages to eat, eat, eat,
    Are not my favourite treat, treat, treat!

Please come and play with me, me, me,
And we will change our tea, tea, tea.
Whatever would suit you, you, you,
We'll make and eat it too, too, too!

♪	D	G	D	E	D	B,
	Please	come	and	play	with	me

4 Puppet people

Tune: My old man's a dustman

Good morning, Mr Beanpole,
Please join us on the floor,
Your head is near the ceiling,
Your shoulders reach the door!

Your looks are really special,
But we don't think you're strange,
We like you just the way you are,
And don't want you to change.

Good morning, Mrs Rainbow,
Please join us on the floor,
Your hair is full of colours,
And sticks out just like straw!

Your looks ...

Good morning, Mr Zigzag,
Please join us on the floor,
Your arms are very zingy,
With springs you can't ignore!

Your looks ...

PSED focus Recognising, celebrating and respecting differences between self and others.

Using the song With paper plates attached to sticks, make three puppets which have distinct features, eg:

Mr Beanpole – a face on a long stick;

Mrs Rainbow – short, spiky multi-coloured paper strips stuck on as hair;

Mr Zigzag – concertina paper limbs.

Use the puppets whilst singing the song to emphasize the uniqueness of the characters.

Have puppets available for the children to use in their free play.

♪ | F♯ | F♯ | F♯ | F♯ | F♯ | F♯ | F♯
Good mor - ning Mis - ter Bean-pole

5 Choosing something different

Tune: Frère Jacques

We wear red socks,
We wear red socks,
We wear grey,
We wear grey,
Choosing something different,
Choosing something different,
That's okay,
That's okay.

We watch TV ...
We're out to play ...
Choosing something different ...
That's okay ...

We like painting ...
We like clay ...

PSED focus Exploring differences and helping children to respect and accept the choices of others.

Using the song This echo song provides you and your class with an instant performance. Divide the children into two groups, one to your left, one to your right. Sing the first line to the first group, who echo you. Turn to the second group and sing the next line to be echoed, and so on through the song.

To remind the children of the words they will be singing, hold up the items you are singing about (or pictures of them) as you sing and while they are echoing you. This will also reinforce the difference between each object or activity.

♪	F	G	A	F
	We	wear	red	socks

6 Who's afraid?

Tune: Goosey, goosey gander

If you're scared of spiders,
If you'd like them banned,
You'll meet other people
Who do not understand.
But we're all scared of something,
We've all had a fright,
So being scared of spiders
Is perfectly alright.

PSED focus Discussing individual dislikes and fears, and ways to reassure each other.

Using the song Identify other dislikes or sources of fear to create new verses.

♪	C	D	C	E	G		G
	If	you're scared of		spi	-		ders

7 Safe and sound

Tune: The animals went in two by two

When Michael came to school today,
   he cried and cried,
He'd lost his teddy on the way,
   he cried and cried,
So then we stopped and looked around,
And teddy turned up safe and sound,
And Michael smiled and
   put his hanky away.

PSED focus Identifying objects that are precious to the children and sharing thoughts and feelings associated with them.

Using the song Collect some 'precious' objects, eg a doll, a teddy, a comic and a moneybox. With the children sitting in a circle, choose a child to select one of the objects and sit in the centre with a tissue. Ask the children to shut their eyes while you hide the chosen object behind a child in the circle. All sing the song while the child in the centre pretends to cry. On the words 'So then we stopped and looked around', the children turn to look behind them. The child nearest the lost item returns it to the child in the middle. The 'finder' becomes the next child to sit in the middle of the circle. Substitute 'Michael' and 'teddy' with the chosen child's name and item.

♪ | B, B, | E E | F♯ G
When Mi - chael came | to school

8 The handy band

Tune: short'nin' bread

Move your fingers, move your hands,

You're all in the handy band.

Jenny tells us how to play,

She's the leader of the band today.

Tapping fingers, that's the way,
Tapping fingers, that's what we'll play.
Tapping fingers, that's the way,
Tapping fingers, that's what we'll play.

PSED focus Developing and demonstrating confidence and ability to lead peers.

Using the song Make a leader's hat by cutting out children's hand shapes and stapling them onto a cardboard band.

Before singing, select a leader to choose a hand action, eg clapping hands, rubbing palms, tapping nails, clicking fingers, drumming fingers, banging fists, fingers tapping together, fingers tickling palm, wiggling fingers (silent), scratching palms, clapping hands back to back.

Sing the song, substituting the leader's name, and making the chosen hand action in lines 5-8, eg

Actions:

Line 1: wiggle fingers then wave hands from side to side;

Line 2: point to everyone round the circle;

Line 3: point to the 'leader';

Line 4: hold hands up to head like the leader's 'crown';

Lines 5-8: follow the leader's hand action.

Choose a new leader and begin the song again.

Ask the child choosing the hand action to say whether they think their action will make a sound.

♪ C' A G A
Move your fin - gers

9 Superhero

Tune: John Brown's body

If I were Superman
  I'd fly across the world,
If I were Superman
  I'd fly across the world,
If I were Superman
  I'd fly across the world,
But I can build a tower.

  I am not a superhero,
  I am not a superhero,
  I am not a superhero,
  But I am proud of me.

If I were Supergirl
  I'd fly out into space ...
But I can sing a song.

  I am not a superhero ...

PSED focus Discussing and celebrating the children's personal achievements.

Using the song Highlight individual children's achievements by making up new lines to replace 'I can build a tower'. Try to find a Superman shirt or cape for the 'achiever' to wear.

Encourage everyone to make 'flying' arm actions during the verses.

♪	D		D	C, B,	D G
	If		I	were Su -	per-man

10 Well done, hip hooray!

Tune: This old man

What a star, what a star,
What a clever clogs you are,
Show us something you have
    done today,
Well done, Simon, hip hooray!

PSED focus Sharing and celebrating achievements.

Using the song After singing the song, a chosen child (Simon) shows the others something they have made or done, eg a painting, tying their laces, etc.

Adapt the third line to suit an occasion when the achievement is something which would be difficult to show, eg counting to ten, playing well together in the playground. For these achievements, sing: 'Tell us something you have learnt today', changing the child's name accordingly.

♪ A F# A   A F# A
What a star, what a star

11 Welcome to a new baby

Tune: My bonnie lies over the ocean

They have a new baby at their house,
They have a new baby at home.
She's tiny and hungry and sleepy,
Their family's suddenly grown.
  Baby Shuma,
  With ten little fingers
    and ten small toes.
  Baby Shuma,
  We welcome you into our world!

PSED focus Welcoming a new family member.

Using the song Invite a parent or carer with a new baby to visit the children so that they can sing this song to them.

As a welcoming gesture, fill in the name of the new baby on the photocopiable page and present it to the family when they visit.

This tune has a strong rocking beat. Let the children rock an imaginary baby, doll or even a bundled towel to the strong beat.

♪	D	B		A	G	A	G
	They	have		a new	ba	-	by

Baby _____,

With ten little fingers
and ten small toes.

Baby _____,

We welcome you into
our world!

12 My best friend has moved away

Tune: London Bridge is falling down

My best friend has moved away,
Moved away, moved away,
My best friend has moved away,
I feel lonely.

Use the phone and ring him now,
Ring him now, ring him now ...
Don't feel lonely.

Write a letter, post it now,
Post it now, post it now ...
Don't feel lonely.

Write an e-mail, send it now,
Send it now, send it now ...
Don't feel lonely.

Mum says he can come to stay,
Come to stay, come to stay ...
I feel better.

My best friend arrives today,
Arrives today, arrives today ...
I'm not lonely.

PSED focus Discussing friendships and ways of keeping in touch with friends who move away.

Using the song Actions will help everyone to remember the words of each verse. First wave goodbye, then pretend to phone, write a letter, type an e-mail, silently cheer or clap, then give yourself a hug.

Ask the children to bring in photos of any friends who have moved away or that have gone to a different school.

♪	A		B	A	G	F♯	G	A
	My		best	friend	has	moved	a -	way

13 Helpers

Tune: There was a farmer had a dog

Let's think of someone that we know,
Who comes along to help us,
    Mrs Singh bakes us cakes,
    Mrs Singh bakes us cakes,
    Mrs Singh bakes us cakes,
She comes along to help us.

PSED focus Acknowledging and building relationships with the various adults who help the children in their setting.

Using the song Before singing, the children decide which helper and job is to be acknowledged. Over time the children can honour all their helpers by making new verses for this song eg, 'Mrs Nicholls sings us songs' or 'Mrs Brownlow mixes paints'.

Give a small group or solo singer the middle repeated lines to make a vocal contrast.

♪	D	G	G	D	D
	Let's	think	of	some - one	

14 When I feel sad

Tune: Aiken Drum

If you smile at me when I feel sad,
Perhaps I won't feel quite so bad,
If you smile at me when I feel sad
Then you'll be a friend to me.

If you talk to me ...

If you'll be my friend ...

If we play a game ...

If you sing with me ...

PSED focus Discussing incidents and events that have made children feel sad.

Using the song From talking about their own experiences, the children may be able to add to the list of sympathetic actions that would cheer someone up.

You may prefer to use incidents from stories in which characters become unhappy, eg 'Dogger' by Shirley Hughes.

♪	A	G	F♯		F♯	F♯
	If	you	smile		at	me

15 Please join in

Tune: There was a princess long ago

Now one will do but two is fun,
Two is fun, two is fun.
Now one will do but two is fun,
Please join in.

Now two will do but four is more,
Four is more, four is more.
Now two will do but four is more,
Please join in.

Now four will do but eight is great,
Eight is great, eight is great.
Now four will do but eight is great,
Please join in.

PSED focus Developing extended friendship groups.

Using the song Make a circle with all children holding hands. Choose one child to stand in the middle whilst the others sing the song. At the end of verse one, the child in the centre chooses a partner to join him or her in the centre. During the next verse, the children in the centre make their own mini-circle and walk round. This continues with the children in the centre choosing new partners at the end of each verse until eight children are in the central circle.

As an alternative to walking round as an inner circle, the children in the centre could choose an instrument to play while the children in the outer circle sing.

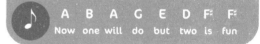

16 My turn, your turn

Tune: Twinkle, twinkle little star

My turn, your turn, we can share,
My turn, your turn, then it's fair.
Make a jigsaw, fun to do,
Then it's time for someone new,
My turn, your turn, we can share,
My turn, your turn, then it's fair.

My turn, your turn, we can share ...
Paint a picture, let it dry,
Someone else can have a try,
My turn, your turn, we can share ...

My turn, your turn, we can share ...
Play dough you can squeeze and bend,
Now you pass it to a friend.
My turn, your turn, we can share ...

PSED focus Turn-taking, sharing and working cooperatively.

Using the song To emphasise the turn-taking message in this song, place a box of jigsaw pieces, a paintbrush, paint pot, rolling pin and a board in the middle of the circle. Choose two children for each verse to go into the centre. Ask the first child to accompany the singing by shaking the jigsaw pieces in the box. When you reach the line 'Now it's time for someone new' the box is passed to the other child who plays along to the singing until the end of the verse. The next pair stir the paint brush in the paint pot, and the last pair roll the rolling pin over the board.

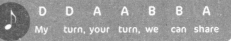

D D A A B B A
My turn, your turn, we can share

17 A job for everyone

Tune: The farmer's in his den

We put the toys away,
We put the toys away,
That's a job for everyone,
We put the toys away.

Pencils in the pot,
Pencils in the pot,
That's a job for everyone,
Pencils in the pot.

Aprons on the hook,
Aprons on the hook,
That's a job for everyone,
Aprons on the hook.

PSED focus Recognising the importance of helping to keep the environment safe and tidy.

Using the song As the song is repetitive and easy to learn, the children can invent new verses, using the day's activities.

Encourage the children to use objects associated with these activities as sound sources. These can be played during the song, eg pencils tapped together, glue spreaders stirred in empty pots, flapping aprons etc.

F♯ A	A B	B A
We put	the toys	a - way

18 We know better

Tune: London Bridge is falling down

Eat your crisps and drop the bag,
Drop the bag, drop the bag?
Eat your crisps and drop the bag?
We know better.

    Put the crisp bag in the bin,
    In the bin, in the bin.
    Put the crisp bag in the bin,
    That's much better.

Chocolate biscuits, eat the lot,
Eat the lot, eat the lot?
Chocolate biscuits, eat the lot?
We know better.

    Take a plate and share them out,
    Share them out, share them out.
    Take a plate and share them out,
    That's much better.

Spill the paint pot, walk away,
Walk away, walk away?
Spill the paint pot, walk away?
We know better.

Find a cloth and mop it up,
Mop it up, mop it up.
Find a cloth and mop it up,
That's much better.

♪ A   B A G F♯ G A
Eat   your crisps and drop the bag?

19 It's a good day

Tune: There's a hole in my bucket

It's a good day for building,
For building, for building,
It's a good day for building,
So what shall we need?

We'll need big bricks and little bricks,
For building, for building,
We'll need big bricks and little bricks,
And that's what we'll need.

It's a good day for dressing-up ...

We'll need big hats and handbags ...

It's a good day for the sand tray ...

We'll need beakers and buckets ...

PSED focus Demonstrating ability to
select the correct equipment for a specific
purpose, collecting and returning it
independently.

Using the song With the children sitting
in a circle, place a pile of the following
objects in the centre:

large and small building bricks;

hats and handbags;

beakers and buckets.

Sing the first verse and then ask two
children to go into the centre to find the
appropriate objects for building while
everyone sings the answering verse.

Invent new verses and ask the children to
find the necessary resources from their
storage places.

G A B D   D E G
It's a good day for build - ing

20 Have another go

Rap

When the b̲ricks fall d̲own,
Tumble d̲own, tumble d̲own,
It m̲akes you f̲rown,
Big f̲rown, big f̲rown.

    Don't s̲tamp your f̲eet,
    Don't t̲hrow things ab̲out,
    Don't g̲et ups̲et,
    Don't s̲cream and s̲hout,
    Just g̲iggle, tee h̲ee!
    Just l̲augh, ho! h̲o!
    Just s̲ort yourself o̲ut
    And h̲ave another g̲o.

When the p̲aint goes sp̲losh!
Wet sp̲losh, wet sp̲losh,
It m̲akes you c̲ross,
So c̲ross, so c̲ross

    Don't s̲tamp your f̲eet ...

PSED focus Learning to cope when things go wrong.

Using the rap Add actions to the repeated section, eg stamping, mimed throwing of objects, hands rubbing away imaginary tears (for being upset). Use really big voices for 'don't scream and shout'.

Once the rap is established, divide the children into two groups, one to speak the words and the other to keep the steady beat by tapping knees or slapping thighs.

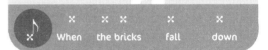

♪	✕	✕ ✕	✕	✕
✕	When	the bricks	fall	down

21 Open wide!

Tune: Little brown jug

Here's the dentist, open wide,
Show all those lovely teeth inside,
Shining, sparkling, clean and bright,
Teeth to talk with, teeth to bite.

Rap:

Hello Sally, come and sit in my chair,
Got your brush and your toothpaste there?
Brush your teeth at the bottom,
Brush your teeth at the top,
Brush your teeth really well,
Rinse your brush and stop!

__ indicates a strong beat

PSED focus Becoming independent and looking after own needs.

Using the song Find a toy (which has visible teeth, eg an alligator or crocodile), a small table and chair, a toothbrush and an empty toothpaste box. Sit in a circle with the table, chair, toy and toothbrush in the centre, passing around the toothpaste box as you sing the song. When the singing ends, the child holding the box sits in the dentist's chair and brushes the toy's teeth while everyone performs the rap.

Recite the rap, showing the children how they can accompany it using body percussion, eg rubbing their palms together on the words 'brush', mime rinsing brushes on 'rinse your brush' and on the word 'stop' pop them into an imaginary holder or glass. Emphasize the strong beats by playing them on a tambour.

♪ C♯ E E E D F♯ F♯
Here's the den - tist, o - pen wide

22 Getting dressed

Tune: See saw, Margery Daw

Push the buttons through the holes,
Can you manage to do it?
Push the buttons through the holes,
You're brilliant, you managed to do it.

Push each finger into your gloves,
Can you manage to do it? ...

Put your socks on, get them straight ...

Do the zip up on your coat ...

PSED focus Learning to dress and undress independently.

Using the song Choose one child for each action mentioned in the song and let them demonstrate, with real clothing, as everyone sings. Reward the achievers with an appropriate sticker.

Invent new verses to match newly-acquired dressing skills, eg tie your laces into bows.

Push the but - tons through the holes
G   G D   D G   G D

23 Soap and bubbles

Tune: Ten green bottles

Soap and bubbles
  wash the germs away,
Soap and bubbles
  wash the germs away.
In the bath or shower
  you splash and have a play,
But soap and bubbles
  wash the germs away.

Bath or shower gel ...

One long loofah ...

Dad's big bath-brush ...

Mum's pink nail-brush ...

PSED focus Discussing the importance of washing and keeping clean.

Using the song Encourage the children to talk about their favourite bathtime products and make a collection of empty packaging which represents these.

Use shampoo bottles containing a little water, nail brushes scraped on corrugated card, or a few cotton buds in a pot to make sounds to accompany the song.

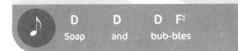

♪	D	D	D F#
	Soap	and	bub-bles

24 Hair do

Rap

Hair can be short,
And hair can be long,
So keep it looking good
And you can't go wrong.

Is it black or brown?
Leave it hanging down.
Is it ginger or red?
Put it up instead.
Is it blond or black?
You can tie it back,
With plaits to make
And beads to shake.

Hair can be short ...

___indicates a strong beat

When you use shampoo,
Then rinse it through.
Give your hair a brush,
Take your time – don't rush.
Use glitter and gel,
And bows as well,
With spikes or curls,
For boys and girls.

Hair can be short ...

25 I can look after me

Chant

I can look after me,
I can look after me.
I'm ever so tough,
I can do lots of stuff,
And I can look after me.

26 Fireworks

Tune: Mary, Mary, quite contrary

Poppers, bangers,
Whizzers and sizzlers,
Squeakers and squealers too.
Our firework music's full of sounds,
That we're going to play for you.

PSED focus Exploring and recognising different festivals and celebrations which use fireworks.

Using the song Divide the children into three firework groups: 'poppers and bangers', 'whizzers and sizzlers' and 'squeakers and squealers'. Within each group, children select instruments or body sounds to represent their two fireworks. After singing the song, the groups take it in turns to perform their firework sounds.

Create a frieze in three sections, portraying the types of fireworks described in the song. This will then act as a score (written music) and remind the children of their compositions as well as being a beautiful piece of artwork.

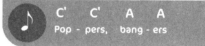

C' C' A A
Pop - pers, bang - ers

27 Party food

Tune: Hot cross buns

Party food, party food,
When you have a celebration,
Party food.
Little pizza slices,
While you're in the mood,
When you have a celebration,
Party food.

PSED focus Exploring the role of food in festivals and celebrations.

Using the song Talk with the children about different kinds of celebratory food, eg birthday teas, Diwali fare, wedding cakes, Christmas dinner etc. Use pictures and food packaging to encourage them to share their memories of celebratory food.

Clap hands together in three positions to show the high, low and middle notes of the repeating line:

par- clap high above your head;
-ty clap near your knees;
food clap near your waist.

Play the phrase 'Party food' on a xylophone. Remove all the bars except high B, low B₁ and E and play these each time the phrase is sung.

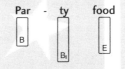

Go shopping for ingredients to make party food and have a wonderful celebration!

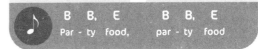

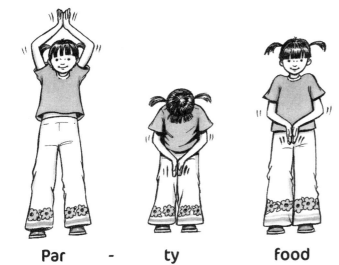

Par   -   ty   food

28 A tasty pancake

Tune: She'll be coming round the mountain

We can make a tasty pancake for our tea,
  yum yum,
We can make a tasty pancake for our tea,
  yum yum,
We can make a tasty pancake,
  make a tasty pancake,
Make a tasty pancake for our tea, yum yum.

yum yum

We'll need eggs and milk and flour
  in a bowl, stir stir ...

Now we'll cook that tasty pancake
  'til it's done, sizzle sizzle ...

We can toss that tasty pancake in the air,
  wheeeeeeee ...

We can share that tasty pancake
  with our friends, chomp chomp ...

stir stir

sizzle sizzle

wheeeeeeee

chomp chomp

PSED Focus Sharing experiences of community celebrations.

Using the song Use different mimed actions for each verse, eg

yum yum – rub tummy;

stir stir – one arm makes a 'bowl' while the other holds a 'spoon' and stirs;

sizzle sizzle – hold a 'frying pan' and wiggle it from side to side;

wheeeee – toss the pancake and make your voice go up and down on 'wheeeeee';

chomp chomp – open and close hands to make a biting action.

Make or buy pancakes for the children and show them pictures of the different festivals when pancakes are eaten:

Shrove Tuesday – a Christian festival when fats and sugars are used up before the period of fasting called Lent;

Hanukah – Jewish families eat potato pancakes called latkes during this autumn festival;

Dutch people eat pannekokke at most festivals and celebrations.

♪ D E G G G G E D
We can make a ta - sty pan - cake

29 Our street

Tune: Twinkle, twinkle little star

See the front doors in a row,
Lots of colours all on show.
Yellow, orange, red and blue,
Green and mauve and turquoise too.
See the front doors in a row,
Lots of colours all on show.

See the gardens in a row,
Lots of colours all on show.
Yellow, orange, red and blue,
Green and mauve and turquoise too.
See the gardens in a row,
Lots of colours all on show.

See the washing in a row,
Lots of colours all on show.
Yellow, orange, red and blue,
Green and mauve and turquoise too.
See the washing in a row,
Lots of colours all on show.

PSED focus Encouraging children to look at the different colours in their environment.

Using the song Talk with the children about their favourite colours and those they have noticed in the environment. Bring in differently coloured objects – garden flowers and items of clothing – and introduce colour sorting activities. If some of your children know the colour of their own front door, incorporate the name of the colour into the first verse of the song.

Line up coloured cards to match the sequence in the song. In the washing verse, line up children wearing the corresponding colours to make a row of washing.

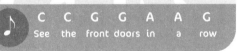

♪ C C G G A A G
♪ See the front doors in a row

30 Friends

Chant and circle game

Friends in the playground,
Friends in the street,
Friends who wave
   whenever you meet.
Friends who are grown-ups,
Friends who are not,
Just think of all the
Friends you've got.

___indicates a strong beat

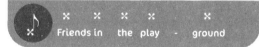

Melody lines

1 First day – Knees up, Mother Brown

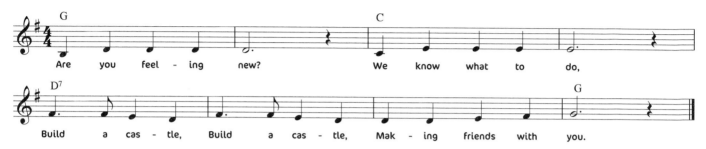

Are you feel – ing new? We know what to do,

Build a cas – tle, Build a cas – tle, Mak – ing friends with you.

2 Special things I do – John Brown's body

I like___ cart – wheels, they're the spe – cial things I do, I like___

cart – wheels, they're the spe – cial things I do, I like___ cart – wheels, they're the

spe – cial things I do, So come and play with me.___

3 Come for tea – A sailor went to sea, sea, sea

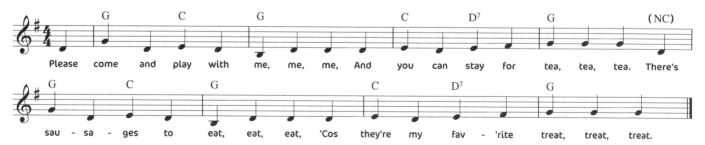

Please come and play with me, me, me, And you can stay for tea, tea, tea. There's

sau – sa – ges to eat, eat, eat, 'Cos they're my fav – 'rite treat, treat, treat.

4 Puppet people – My old man's a dustman

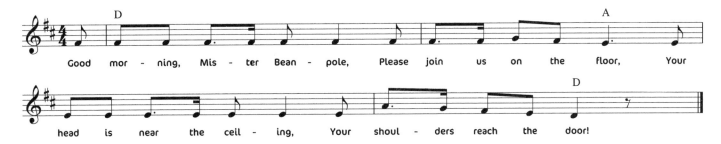

Good mor - ning, Mis - ter Bean - pole, Please join us on the floor, Your

head is near the ceil - ing, Your shoul - ders reach the door!

5 Choosing something different – Frère Jacques

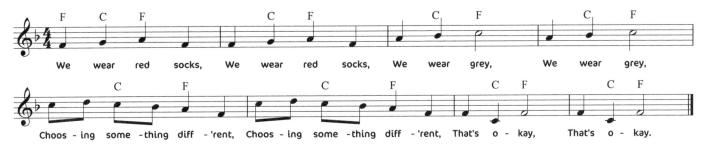

We wear red socks, We wear red socks, We wear grey, We wear grey,

Choos - ing some -thing diff - 'rent, Choos - ing some -thing diff - 'rent, That's o - kay, That's o - kay.

6 Who's afraid? – Goosey, goosey gander

If you're scared of spi - ders, If you'd like them banned, You'll meet oth - er peo - ple Who do not un - der -stand, But

we're all scared of some -thing, We've all had a fright, So be -ing scared of spi - ders Is per -fect -ly al -right.

7 Safe and sound – The animals went in two by two

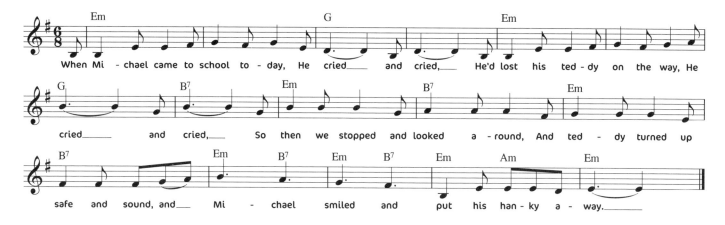

When Mi – chael came to school to – day, He cried___ and cried,___ He'd lost his ted – dy on the way, He cried___ and cried,___ So then we stopped and looked a – round, And ted – dy turned up safe and sound, and___ Mi – chael smiled and put his han – ky a – way.___

8 The handy band – short'nin' bread

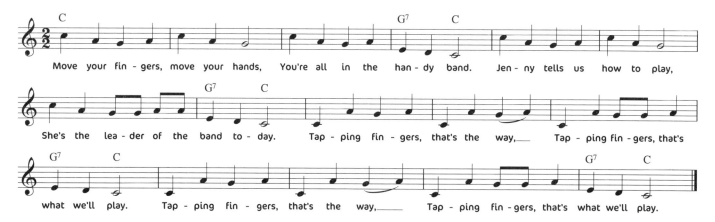

Move your fin – gers, move your hands, You're all in the han – dy band. Jen – ny tells us how to play, She's the lea – der of the band to – day. Tap – ping fin – gers, that's the way,___ Tap – ping fin – gers, that's what we'll play. Tap – ping fin – gers, that's the way,___ Tap – ping fin – gers, that's what we'll play.

9 Superhero – John Brown's body

If I were Su-per-man I'd fly a-cross the world, If I were Su-per-man I'd fly a-cross the world,

If I were Su-per-man I'd fly a-cross the world, But I can build a tower.____

I am not a su-per-he – ro, I am not a su-per-he – ro,

I am not a su-per-he – ro, But I am proud of me.____

10 Well done, hip hooray! – This old man

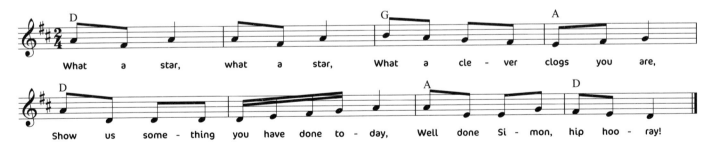

What a star, what a star, What a cle – ver clogs you are,

Show us some – thing you have done to – day, Well done Si – mon, hip hoo – ray!

11 Welcome to a new baby – My bonnie lies over the ocean

They have a new ba-by at their house,_ They have a new ba-by at home._ She's

ti-ny and hun-gry and sleep-y,_ Their fa-mi-ly's sud-den-ly grown._ Ba-

by Shu – ma, With ten lit-tle fin-gers and ten small toes.

Ba – by Shu – ma, We wel-come you in-to our world!_

12 My best friend has moved away– London Bridge is falling down

My best friend has moved a – way, Moved a – way, moved a – way,

My best friend has moved a – way, I feel lone – ly.

13 Helpers – There was a farmer had a dog

Let's think of some-one that we know, Who comes a-long to help us, Mis-sis Singh bakes us cakes,

Mis-sis Singh bakes us cakes, Mis-sis Singh bakes us cakes, She comes a-long to help us.

14 When I feel sad – Aiken Drum

If you smile at me when I feel sad, Per-haps I won't feel quite so bad, If you

smile at me when I feel sad Then you'll be a friend to me.

15 Please join in – There was a princess long ago

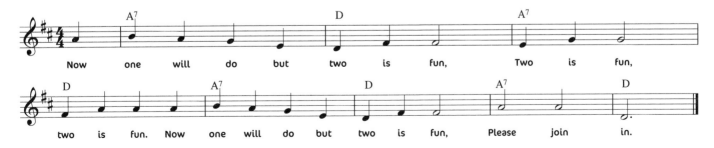

Now one will do but two is fun, Two is fun,

two is fun. Now one will do but two is fun, Please join in.

16 My turn, your turn – Twinkle, twinkle little star

My turn, your turn, we can share, My turn, your turn, then it's fair, Make a jig - saw, fun to do!

Then it's time for some – one new, My turn, your turn, we can share, My turn, your turn, then it's fair.

17 A job for everyone – The farmer's in his den

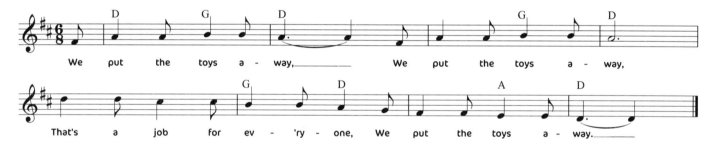

We put the toys a - way,_____ We put the toys a - way,

That's a job for ev - 'ry - one, We put the toys a - way._____

18 We know better – London Bridge is falling down

Eat your crisps and drop the bag, Drop the bag, drop the bag?

Eat your crisps and drop the bag? We know bet - ter.

19 It's a good day – There's a hole in my bucket

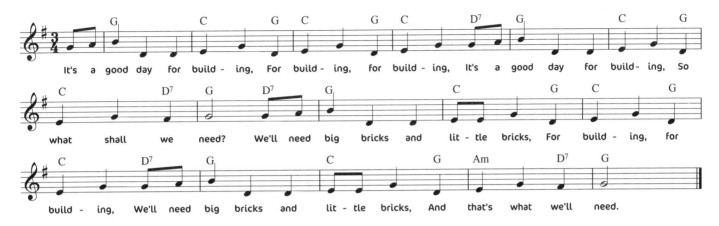

It's a good day for build – ing, For build – ing, for build – ing, It's a good day for build – ing, So what shall we need? We'll need big bricks and lit – tle bricks, For build – ing, for build – ing, We'll need big bricks and lit – tle bricks, And that's what we'll need.

20 Have another go – Rap

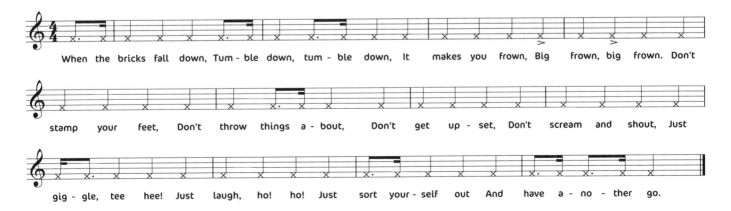

When the bricks fall down, Tum – ble down, tum – ble down, It makes you frown, Big frown, big frown. Don't stamp your feet, Don't throw things a – bout, Don't get up – set, Don't scream and shout, Just gig – gle, tee hee! Just laugh, ho! ho! Just sort your – self out And have a – no – ther go.

21 Open wide! – Little brown jug

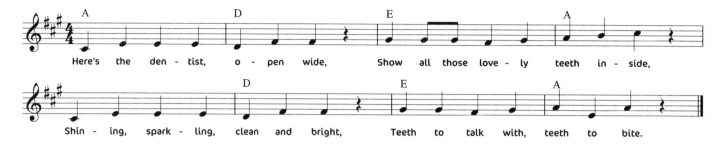

Here's the den - tist, o - pen wide, Show all those love - ly teeth in - side,

Shin - ing, spark - ling, clean and bright, Teeth to talk with, teeth to bite.

21 Open wide! – Rap

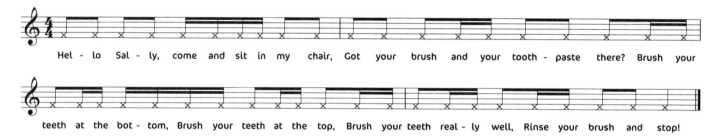

Hel - lo Sal - ly, come and sit in my chair, Got your brush and your tooth - paste there? Brush your

teeth at the bot - tom, Brush your teeth at the top, Brush your teeth real - ly well, Rinse your brush and stop!

22 Getting dressed – See saw, Margery Daw

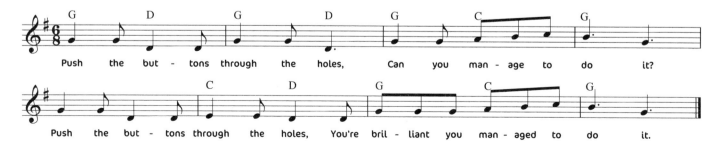

Push the but - tons through the holes, Can you man - age to do it?

Push the but - tons through the holes, You're bril - liant you man - aged to do it.

23 Soap and bubbles – Ten green bottles

Soap and bub-bles___ wash the germs a-way, Soap and bub-bles___ wash the germs a-way. In the
bath or show-er,___ you splash and have a play, But soap and bub-bles___ wash the germs a-way.

24 Hair do – Rap

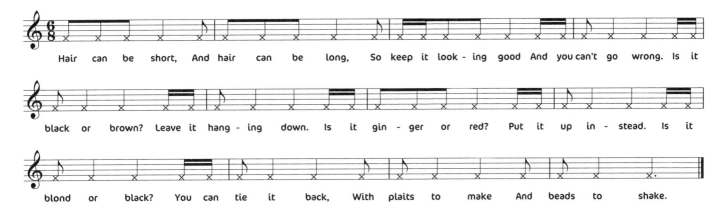

Hair can be short, And hair can be long, So keep it look-ing good And you can't go wrong. Is it
black or brown? Leave it hang-ing down. Is it gin-ger or red? Put it up in-stead. Is it
blond or black? You can tie it back, With plaits to make And beads to shake.

25 I can look after me – Chant

I can look af – ter me, I can look af – ter me. I'm

e – ver so tough, I can do lots of stuff, And I can look af – ter me.

26 Fireworks – Mary, Mary, quite contrary

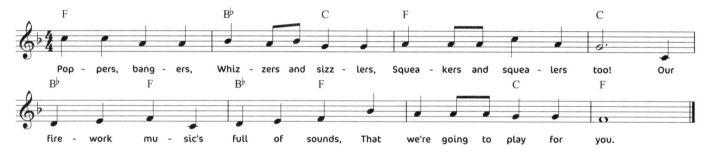

Pop – pers, bang – ers, Whiz – zers and sizz – lers, Squea – kers and squea – lers too! Our

fire – work mu – sic's full of sounds, That we're going to play for you.

27 Party food – Hot cross buns

Par – ty food, par – ty food, When you have a ce – le – bra – tion, Par – ty food.

Lit – tle piz – za sli – ces, While you're in the mood, When you have a ce – le – bra – tion, Par – ty food.

28 We can make a tasty pancake – She'll be coming round the mountain

We can make a tas – ty pan-cake for our tea, yum yum, We can make a tas – ty pan cake for our tea, yum yum, We can

make a tas – ty pan-cake, Make a tas – ty pan-cake, Make a tas – ty pan-cake for our tea, yum yum.

29 Our street – Twinkle, twinkle little star

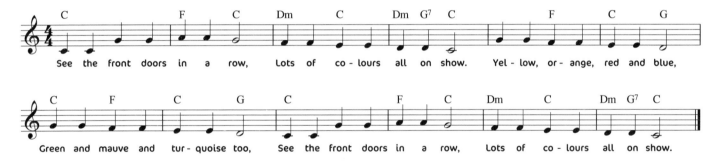

See the front doors in a row, Lots of co – lours all on show. Yel – low, or – ange, red and blue,

Green and mauve and tur – quoise too, See the front doors in a row, Lots of co – lours all on show.

30 Friends – Chant and circle game

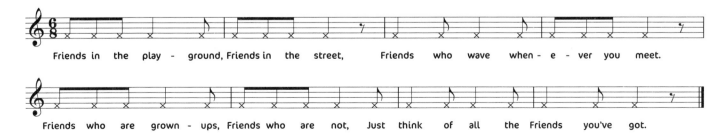

Friends in the play – ground, Friends in the street, Friends who wave when – e – ver you meet.

Friends who are grown – ups, Friends who are not, Just think of all the Friends you've got.

Index

More music for young children from A & C Black ...

Bobby Shaftoe, clap your hands

Developing basic music skills with new songs from old favourites for 3–7 year olds.

Three tapping teddies

Familiar and new stories with songs, raps and ways into music for 3–5 year olds.

Let's go Zudie-o

Creative activities for dance and music exploration for 3–5 year olds.

Bingo lingo

Supporting language development for 4-7 year olds with songs and rhymes.

Tom Thumb's musical maths

Supporting numeracy for 4-7 year olds with songs and rhymes.

High low dolly pepper

A comprehensive resource of activities for establishing the basics of music with 4-7 year olds.

Livelytime Playsongs

Baby's active day in songs and colourful pictures – with full CD performances – for 0–3 year olds.

Sleepytime Playsongs

Baby's restful day in songs and colourful pictures – with full CD performances – for 0–3 year olds.